D1038879

PRAY

Talk to the King of the Universe

Kevin Johnson

DEEPER SERIES

PRAY

Talk to the King of the Universe

Kevin Johnson

ZONDERVAN®

ZONDERVAN.com/
AUTHORTRACKER
follow your favorite authors

youth
specialties

**youth
specialties**

Pray: Talk to the King of the Universe
Copyright 2007 by Kevin Johnson

Youth Specialties resources, 300 S. Pierce St., El Cajon, CA 92020 are published by
Zondervan, 5300 Patterson Ave. SE, Grand Rapids, MI 49530.

Library of Congress Cataloging-in-Publication Data

Johnson, Kevin (Kevin Walter)
  Pray : talk to the king of the universe / by Kevin Johnson.
     p. cm.
  ISBN-10: 0-310-27492-3 (pbk.)
  ISBN-13: 978-0-310-27492-6 (pbk.)
  1. Prayer—Biblical teaching—Juvenile literature. 2.
Prayer—Christianity—Juvenile literature. I. Title.
  BV212.J65 2007
  248.3'2—dc22

                                                                    2007039355

Web site addresses listed in this book were current at the time of publication. Please
contact Youth Specialties via e-mail (YS@YouthSpecialties.com) to report URLs that
are no longer operational and replacement URLs if available.

Cover and interior design by SharpSeven Design

Printed in the United States of America

---

07 08 09 10 11 12 • 20 19 18 17 16 15 14 13 12 11 10 9 8 7 6 5 4 3 2 1

Contents

Start Here

It's cool that you're cracking open this book. If you've ever wanted to dig into the Bible or find out what it takes to grow in your faith, the DEEPER series is like an enormous neon finger that'll point you toward exactly what you need to know.

Pray contains 20 Bible studies that build piece by piece. You'll check out Scripture, think for yourself, and feed on insights you might not otherwise find. Consider this your own personal manual on prayer—a guide to help you know not only how to pray, but also why you'd want to. You'll discover that God really does want to give you good gifts. You'll dig into the tough parts of prayer, like why some of your requests seem to go unanswered. And you'll find that prayer is having a conversation with the One who knows you best and loves you most.

Don't rush. Pick your own pace—from a study per day to a study per week. Actually, the slower you go, the more you'll gain. While each study is just a couple of pages long, every one of them is tagged with another page of bonus material that can help you dig even deeper.

Each study opens with a mostly blank page that has a single Bible verse that sums up the main point. These verses are worth memorizing, as a way to lock your head on to the awesome truths of God's Word. Then comes **START**, a brief intro to get your brain geared up for the topic. **READ** takes you to a short Scripture passage. You can read it here in the book or, if you want, grab your own Bible and read the passage there. **THINK** helps you examine the main ideas of the passage, and **LIVE** makes it easy to apply what you learn. **WRAP** pulls everything together.

Then there's that bonus material. **MORE THOUGHTS TO MULL** tosses you a few more questions to ask yourself or others. **MORE SCRIPTURES TO DIG** leads you to related Bible passages to get you the full scoop on a topic.

Whether you read on your own or get together with a group, *Pray* will help you take your next step in becoming wildly devoted to Jesus. If you're ready to grab hold of a heart-to-heart, all-out relationship with God, dig in!

1. COME AND DINE

The real purpose of prayer

Revelation 3:20

"Here I am! I stand at the door and knock.

If anyone hears my voice and opens the door,

I will come in and eat with them, and they with me."

➜   **START** Some people think prayer is like ordering a pizza. You dial up God and rattle off what you want. If all goes well, a few minutes later you're devouring a snack made exactly the way you like it. But God has a totally different angle on prayer. He's no underpaid delivery guy who drops off the goods, drives away, then kills time at the shop waiting for your next order. When God shows up at your door with a jumbo-sized deep dish supreme, he wants to come in and eat.

When do you pray? What do you say when you talk to God?

➜   **READ** Revelation 3:20

Jesus said: [20]"Here I am! I stand at the door and knock. If anyone hears my voice and opens the door, I will come in and eat with them, and they with me."

➜   **THINK** This verse shows up in the last book of the Bible, in a section of short letters where Jesus challenges the early Christians to grab hold of true faith. The passage is about more than prayer. It's an amazing picture of how Jesus aims to get along with us.

That's Jesus rapping his knuckles on "the door." At what door is he knocking?

What two things do you need to do to accept this dinner invite from Jesus? Then what will he do?

Why would Jesus pick eating together as a picture of his relationship with us?

Sharing a lunch table can show people who your friends are, although sometimes you end up sitting with someone you might rather ditch. Back in Bible times there were strict rules detailing whom you could eat with—or not. Sharing food was a deep public sign of friendship and approval.

➜ **LIVE** How is prayer nothing like ordering a pizza? And how is God unlike a pizza delivery person?

Brainstorm a list of ways that prayer is like sitting down to dine with Jesus.

This book will walk you through a wild variety of Bible prayers, but they all come down to this: Prayer is having a conversation with the One who knows you best and loves you most. It's your chance to talk with him at any moment about every part of life.

If Jesus knocked on your head and your heart and said, "I want to get to know you, and I want you to know me," how would you respond?

→   **WRAP** It's a promise: If you open the door to God, he guarantees that he'll walk right in. And every time you open your mouth to pray, you're grabbing an opportunity to know God better. Whenever you pray, you get far more than whatever slab of crust, meat, and oozing cheese you're hoping for. You get God himself.

»   MORE THOUGHTS TO MULL

- When have you talked to God as if he shuttles pizzas for a living? When in your life has prayer been bigger than that?

- Picture yourself sitting down to eat with Jesus. Where are you eating? What's on the menu? Why do you picture that?

- The artist Holman Hunt (1827-1910) was so inspired by Revelation 3:20 that he painted "The Light of the World," a classic picture showing Jesus knocking at a door overgrown with weeds. Google the image and take a good look at it. Someone once told Hunt he'd goofed because he'd forgotten to paint a handle on the outside of the door. Holman answered that it was no mistake. "There's only one handle," he said, "and it's on the inside." Question: What does it mean that the door of your life can only be opened from the inside?

- Pray it: *God, I don't just want the good things you can give me. I want you.*

» MORE SCRIPTURES TO DIG

- Flip to **Matthew 9:9-13**, **Luke 7:36-50**, and **Luke 19:1-9** to glimpse real-life pictures of Jesus eating with people. Notice how Jesus doesn't try to impress a popular host—such as the Pharisee in Luke 7—but he goes out of his way to eat with ordinary people. If Jesus had followed the rules laid down by the religious leaders of his day, he wouldn't have gone near sinners like tax collectors and prostitutes. For that matter, he wouldn't have sat down to eat with any of us.

- Check the background of Revelation 3:20 by reading the verses right around it, **Revelation 3:14-22**. The Christians in Laodicea were like the lukewarm waters of their town—neither hot like the healing springs just to the north, nor cold like the refreshing waters found to the southeast. Jesus says he will spew them from his mouth if they continue to settle for mediocrity in their relationship with him.

- God's people used food to celebrate their connection with him long before church potlucks were invented. In fact, the Bible is jammed with references to food, fun, and deep fellowship. You'll find several descriptions of Old Testament festivals in **Leviticus 23**. And in **Psalm 23:5** God spreads a feast for the great King David while David's enemies look on. Jesus tells his followers to remember him with a sacred meal, the Lord's Supper, in **1 Corinthians 11:23-26**. And in **Revelation 19:7-10** the celebration in heaven kicks off with the wedding supper of the Lamb.

2. ASK AND KEEP ASKING

God likes your prayers

Matthew 7:7

"Ask and it will be given to you; seek and you will find;

knock and the door will be opened to you."

➜ **START** When ancient Egyptians buried a dead body, they packed the tomb with all the treasure and trinkets a person would need after death—as if a mummy would need much. God doesn't plan to fill your coffin and fly you to the land of the dead. He wants to set you up with everything you need to survive and thrive in life. Here's a shocking fact: You don't have to beg to get God to give. He doesn't just permit you to ask. He *tells* you to.

Sometimes you pray and get what you want, yet maybe more often you don't. So do you think God likes to give to you, or do you think he's basically stingy? Explain your answer.

➜ **READ** Matthew 7:7-11

> Jesus said: ⁷"Ask and it will be given to you; seek and you will find; knock and the door will be opened to you. ⁸For everyone who asks receives; those who seek find; and to those who knock, the door will be opened. ⁹Which of you, if your son asks for bread, will give him a stone? ¹⁰Or if he asks for a fish, will give him a snake? ¹¹If you, then, though you are evil, know how to give good gifts to your children, how much more will your Father in heaven give good gifts to those who ask him!"

➜ **THINK** Those three verbs—*ask, seek,* and *knock*—are in a tense that means "do it and keep doing it." What will happen if you...

• Ask?

• Seek?

• Knock?

Jesus wants his listeners to grasp God's eagerness to give. So he whips out an analogy, pointing to human parents to illustrate God's goodness. How do moms and dads react when their kids ask for what they need?

How is that reaction similar to or different from God's?

Your parents probably don't grant you every wish on your Christmas list nor run out and buy every single item you point out when you walk through a mall. You also know that some human parents commit acts of massive cruelty and abuse toward their children. Yet most moms and dads wisely provide for their kids. They wouldn't think of giving a child a rock masquerading as bread or a chunk of anything deadly.

What gifts do you think God wants to give to you? What good things might he want to give you that don't come with a price tag?

➔   **LIVE** Jesus makes bold promises here. What surprises you about what he says? What parts are tough to believe?

Say it in your own words: How eager is God to hear your prayers and meet your needs?

➡ **WRAP** If prayer meant you always got exactly what you asked for, then you might be driving a red Lamborghini and living in a house with its own zip code. Yet God does tell you to ask boldly for what you need. When he sends his answers, he doesn't play tricks. He's smart enough to give you only his best.

» MORE THOUGHTS TO MULL

- When have you prayed and seen an answer right away?

- Have you ever asked God for something and had trouble understanding why God said no or the prayer seemed to go unanswered? If you're thinking about something enormously tough, keep reading *Pray* to understand more about how prayer works. And ask a pastor or youth director for help in understanding how God answers our requests.

- Pray it: *God, help me trust that you want to give me great gifts.*

» MORE SCRIPTURES TO DIG

- God has a heap of everything you need in life, from material stuff to emotional strength and even spiritual wisdom. **Matthew 6:24-34** says God knows your every physical need. **Philippians 4:13** reminds you that God's power enables you to do whatever you need to do in life. **James 1:5-7** asserts that God provides guidance for anyone committed to doing his will. And **Philippians 4:19** sums it all up: "My God will meet all your needs according to the riches of his glory in Christ Jesus."

- When you pray, you're not begging from a stranger. You're talking to your Father in heaven. And what he has for you is great—as flawless as his love for you. **James 1:17** says, "Every good and perfect gift is from above, coming down from the Father of the heavenly lights, who does not change like shifting shadows."

- Don't ever think that you pray to a grouch. Jesus told a wild story about a guy who goes to a friend's house in the middle of the night, bangs on the door, and asks to borrow some bread to feed his unexpected house guest. "Can't you tell the doors are locked? We're all in bed!" the bugged friend hollers back. Yet the man got up to give his friend what he needed. If humans can manage to be generous in the middle of the night, Jesus said, then we can be sure that God is truly eager to give (**Luke 11:5-8**).

3. ALL THESE THINGS

God knows what you need

Matthew 6:31-32

"So do not worry, saying, 'What shall we eat?' or 'What shall we drink?' or 'What shall we wear?'

For the pagans run after all these things, and your heavenly Father knows that you need them."

➔   **START** Hannah never anticipated that she'd feel such a jolt after returning home from a mission trip to a blistering hot village thousands of miles away. Meeting dirty, barely clothed kids who lived in tin shacks had messed with her ideas of what matters most in life. She liked the comfort of her stuff back home, but she felt she didn't need all of it. And sometimes she felt selfish asking God for things that suddenly seemed petty.

How do you tell the difference between a need and a want? What difference does that make in what you pray for?

➔   **READ** Matthew 6:28-33

Jesus said: [28]"And why do you worry about clothes? See how the flowers of the field grow. They do not labor or spin. [29]Yet I tell you that not even Solomon in all his splendor was dressed like one of these. [30]If that is how God clothes the grass of the field, which is here today and tomorrow is thrown into the fire, will he not much more clothe you—you of little faith? [31]So do not worry, saying, 'What shall we eat?' or 'What shall we drink?' or 'What shall we wear?' [32]For the pagans run after all these things, and your heavenly Father knows that you need them. [33]But seek first his kingdom and his righteousness, and all these things will be given to you as well."

➔   **THINK** That's Jesus talking. What all does he say not to worry about?

A "pagan" is someone who doesn't bow to the one true God and often follows multiple gods. To "run after" is a really strong form of the term *seek*. What's the problem with chasing "all these things"?

Why don't you need to worry about these things—or for that matter, anything else you need?

➜ **LIVE** Do you think God actually understands what you need? Why—or why not?

Consider these facts: God assembled you in your mom's womb (Psalm 139:13-15). He knows the schedule for your entire life (Psalm 139:16). He reads every thought in your brain (Psalm 139:2), and he counts every hair on your head (Matthew 10:30). He even grasps what it's like to live in your skin because Jesus, who is totally God, came to earth as a human being (John 1:14).

If God knows you up close and personal—and can spot exactly what you need—how does that change how you talk to him?

Think of a need you have. It can be tiny or huge. It can be something physical and concrete, or something invisible (like strength or courage). Maybe it's a need that you've never dared share with anyone else. What do you want to tell God about that?

➜ **WRAP** God comprehends everything you need, whether it's help with your homework, freedom from sin, or money for your next meal. Put God first, and he takes care of the rest. Like it says at the end of this passage, "Seek first his kingdom and his righteousness, and all these things will be given to you as well."

❯❯ MORE THOUGHTS TO MULL

- The Bible says God knows exactly what you need even before a request leaves your lips (Matthew 6:8). So why bother to pray?

- What do you wish you had that you don't—or what stuff do you think you need in order to fit in with your peers? How do those desires affect what you pray for?

- Is it wrong to ask God for luxuries—or for little things? Explain.

- Pray it: *God, thanks for taking care of all my needs.*

❯❯ MORE SCRIPTURES TO DIG

- Check out this whole Bible passage, **Matthew 6:19-34**. The words you read above build on a simple point: There's more to life than stuff because your real treasure is in heaven.

- The Bible's message about money and all the things it can buy isn't as simple as "stuff is always bad" or "stuff is always good." Some key thoughts: Good gifts come from God (**James 1:17**). God blesses you with abundance (**Psalm 23:5**). God wants you to dedicate what you have to him (**1 Timothy 4:4-5**). While you're at it, say thanks for all you've been given (**1 Thessalonians 5:18**). Possessions aren't the most important things in life (**Matthew 16:26**). If you fall in love with stuff, then you're not fully in love with God (**1 John 2:15-17**).

- You've no doubt heard people say that "money is the root of all evil" as if they pulled that saying straight out of the Bible. What Scripture actually says is that "the *love* of money is *a* root of *all kinds of* evil" (**1 Timothy 6:10**, emphasis added). That same Bible passage also explains why we can't fall in love with cold hard cash and all the things it can buy: "Those who want to get rich fall into temptation and a trap and into many foolish and harmful desires that plunge people into ruin and destruction" (**1 Timothy 6:9**).

- God made gold, and gold is good. But back in the Old Testament, God's people made a good thing bad. They melted their gold jewelry, cast a statue of a baby cow, and bowed down to worship it (**Exodus 32:1-35**). Notice that the people made the golden calf the minute they stopped believing God cared for them. It sounds incredibly goofy until we realize we still find ways to do the same thing. Whenever we let something get bigger than God in our lives, we've made an idol. We're busting the first commandment, which says, "I am the Lord your God...You shall have no other gods before me" (**Exodus 20:2-3**).

4. CAN YOU HEAR ME NOW?

Ask according to God's will

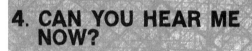

1 John 5:14

This is the confidence we have in approaching God:

that if we ask anything according to his will, he hears us.

➜   **START** God doesn't lounge around with a gigantic cell phone glued to his ear. So you don't have to worry that your calls to him will get dropped if you take a wrong step to the left or the right. Still, there's a zone you want to stay inside if you want him to answer your prayers. The Bible says God hears your prayers when they line up with his will☐ his amazing plans for you and for the rest of the world.

Have you ever prayed but felt unsure God was really listening? What was that like?

➜   **READ** 1 John 5:14-15

> ¹⁴This is the confidence we have in approaching God: that if we ask anything according to his will, he hears us. ¹⁵And if we know that he hears us—whatever we ask—we know that we have what we asked of him.

➜   **THINK** In this passage, the phrase "he hears us" doesn't just mean our request has reached God loud and clear. It means our prayer is "heard favorably." So when can you be confident about asking God for something?

What's a will? (Hint: When someone dies, what does a will accomplish?)

How might you figure out what God's will is—so you can ask for the right things?

God doesn't want you to guess about his will. This is a thick subject, but there are some easy-to-grasp main points. God has—

> • An "ultimate" will. He wants you to believe in and follow him. "God our Savior...wants all people to be saved and to come to a knowledge of the truth" (1 Timothy 2:3-4).

> • A "universal" will. He wants you to obey the Bible's commands, instructions he intends for everyone. Jesus said, "You are my friends if you do what I command" (John 15:14).

> • A "specific" will. He wants you to live by the step-by-step personal guidance he offers you through the Bible, prayer, circumstances, and wise advice. "In all your ways submit to him, and he will make your paths straight" (Proverbs 3:6).

By the way, sometimes God doesn't make his will as clear as a brightly lit billboard. What then? Put God first and ask for what you think is best: "Take delight in the Lord and he will give you the desires of your heart" (Psalm 37:4). (Look for more on getting a grip on God's will in Study 17.)

➜   **LIVE** You've no doubt caught the gist of this passage—when you pray, you should think about what God wants, not just what you want. How hard is that?

If you pray for what God wants—his will—do you believe you'll always get what you ask for? Why—or why not?

God's promise is clear. He guarantees to grant us what we ask for when we ask according to his will. Yet our view of God's plans can be blurry— that is, we don't always perfectly understand what he wants. However, when you get to know God and what the Bible says about his awesome plans for your life, you'll have a better idea of his will. Your requests will better match his plans for you.

➡️ **WRAP** God *wants* you to discover his will. He *wants* you to ask for all of those good things. And when you ask for God's will—whatever it is—you're going to get God's best.

» MORE THOUGHTS TO MULL

- When you pray, how often do you think about what God wants, not just what *you* want?

- Say you want to pray for a friend. How can you figure out God's will for someone else—and pray it?

- Suppose you decide to totally follow God—to desire his will in every part of your life. What would that be like?

- Pray it: *God, I want you. And I want all of your will in my life.*

» MORE SCRIPTURES TO DIG

- **Psalm 37:3-7** teaches great tips for getting in the zone of God's will. It teaches you how to "take delight in the Lord" and "commit your way" to him.

- **Jeremiah 29:11** leaves no doubt about how good it is to follow God's map for your life: " 'For I know the plans I have for you,' declares the Lord, 'plans to prosper you and not to harm you, plans to give you hope and a future.' "

- The Old Testament passage **Psalm 40:7-8** says, "Then I said, 'Here I am, I have come—it is written about me in the scroll. I desire to do your will, my God; your law is within my heart.' " Flip to **Hebrews 10:5-10** to see who that verse is applied to in the New Testament.

- Jesus says we'll get what we ask for when we pray in his name (**John 14:13; 15:16**), and you've likely heard people finish their prayers with "in Jesus' name, Amen." That isn't a magic formula. It's another way of praying according to his will. The Bible also coaches us that our prayers will be effective when we stick close to Jesus (**John 15:7**) and obey his commands (**1 John 3:21-22**).

5. THE HEART OF THE MATTER

Pray for the right reason

James 4:3

When you ask, you do not receive, because you ask with wrong motives,

that you may spend what you get on your pleasures.

➔   **START** God has piles of good gifts. If he's so eager to share, then you've got to wonder why you don't always and instantly get whatever you ask for. Well, just because you plop a desire in front of God, that doesn't mean it would be the smartest idea in the universe for him to say yes! For starters, God won't give you anything evil or hurtful. There are also things he won't do, like forcing divorcing parents back together against their wills. You might be craving the right thing at the wrong time. Or sometimes your attitude just needs rearranging.

When have you prayed really hard for something, yet your motives weren't so good?

➔   **READ** James 4:1-4

¹What causes fights and quarrels among you? Don't they come from your desires that battle within you? ²You desire but do not have, so you kill. You covet but you cannot get what you want, so you quarrel and fight. You do not have because you do not ask God. ³When you ask, you do not receive, because you ask with wrong motives, that you may spend what you get on your pleasures. ⁴You adulterous people, don't you know that friendship with the world means enmity against God? Anyone who chooses to be a friend of the world becomes an enemy of God.

➔   **THINK** Why do people fight?

James suggests it's better to ask for what we need than to fight with other people. Then he makes another strong comment. When people do go to God, why does James say they sometimes don't get what they want?

The New Testament was originally written in Greek. And the Greek word for "desires" gives us our word *hedonism,* a four-syllable way to say you seek pleasure above everything else in life. The phrase "to spend what you get" is the same label the Bible uses for the way a disobedient son trashed his life and money (Luke 15:14).

Wanting to satisfy only yourself—instead of helping others and pleasing God—is "adulterous." Why does selfishness deserve such a nasty label?

God is so jealous for your love that your selfishness is like hopping in bed with someone else's spouse. God wants you to resist whatever pulls you away from him, whether it's outright evil or anything that's not totally good.

➜   **LIVE** This Bible passage hints that we don't ask God *often enough.* What keeps you from going to God for what you need?

Think of the last two or three things you've asked God for. What were they? What motivated your requests?

Think positive. What motivations would God think are great reasons to pray for something? List a bunch.

➡   **WRAP** God is eager to answer your prayers, but not just because you pray for the right things. He wants you to pray for the right things *for the right reasons.*

»   MORE THOUGHTS TO MULL

- Why would God want your attitude to be right before he drops some enormous blessing in your lap?

- When have you been in trouble with authorities in your life — parents, teachers, coaches — because your attitude was ugly? Why was your attitude such a major deal?

- When has your attitude made it smooth to get along with those same people?

- Pray it: *God, reshape the things I want from you. Help me want the right things for the right reasons.*

» MORE SCRIPTURES TO DIG

- Fights between people go all the way back to the dawn of human history—and they always spill over into how people get along with God. In **Genesis 3:1-24** Adam and Eve battle each other and end up hiding from God. When Cain kills his brother in **Genesis 4:1-16,** his self-centeredness makes him mouthy toward the Lord.

- The Bible tells us to look hard at the heart-attitude behind our actions. Jesus rattled off all kinds of wicked stuff that starts in the heart: "evil thoughts, murder, adultery, sexual immorality, theft, false testimony, slander" (**Matthew 15:19**). Like **Proverbs 4:23** says, "Above all else, guard your heart, for everything you do flows from it."

- Jesus said our attitudes always show in our words: "For out of the overflow of the heart the mouth speaks" (**Matthew 12:34**). His point applies not just to what we say to others, but also how we talk to God.

- If your attitudes feel like a mess, ask God to help. **Psalm 139:23-24** shows us how to ask God to check out our hearts. **Psalm 51:10** helps you ask him to make it right. (Catch more on these verses in Study 8.)

6. SAY IT LIKE JESUS

Pray God's way

Luke 11:1

One day Jesus was praying in a certain place.

When he finished, one of his disciples said to him, "Lord, teach us to pray."

➜ **START** A firm grasp on Cole's shoulder steers him toward the microphone. "They're waiting for you," his youth pastor whispers. Without warning, the crushing pressure of praying in front of the entire church mutates the language centers of Cole's adolescent brain into those of a sixteenth-century English churchman: "Holiest Father who arteth in heaveneth," Cole intones, "we thanketh thee for thy trulyeth bounteous gifts unto we, and prayeth thy divine beneficent and magnificent blessings upon us, thy humbleth servants. Verily and verily, Ah-men."

How are you supposed to talk when you pray?

➜ **READ** Luke 11:1-4

¹One day Jesus was praying in a certain place. When he finished, one of his disciples said to him, "Lord, teach us to pray, just as John taught his disciples." ²He said to them, "When you pray, say: 'Father, hallowed be your name, your kingdom come. ³Give us each day our daily bread. ⁴Forgive us our sins, for we also forgive everyone who sins against us. And lead us not into temptation.' "

➜ **THINK** To whom does Jesus tell his followers to pray?

Jesus' calling God "Father" might not surprise you if you've heard these words of Jesus all your life. But it should shock you. Jesus doesn't pray to the "the-God-who-lives-at-the-other-end-of-the-universe" or "the-earth-scorching-people-hating God" or even "the-give-me-what-I-want-right-now God." He calls out to his Father, a respectful yet tight relationship.

Make a list of the things Jesus says we can pray for.

People have noticed that Jesus' prayer has four parts: praise (honoring God), repentance (asking for forgiveness), asking (the daily bread and dealing with temptation parts), and yielding (telling God you want his will). If you take the first letter of those four key words and roll them all together, they spell PRAY. (More on those parts of prayer in the next four studies of *Pray*.)

➡   **LIVE** From everything you've learned so far in life, how do you think you're supposed to pray? How is that prayer the same or different from the sort of prayer Jesus taught?

Rate each of the following from 1 to 10 (1 = "incredibly uncomfortable" and 10 = "incredibly easy"). Explain why.

_____ Praying by yourself
_____ Praying with other people
_____ Praying silently
_____ Praying out loud

When have you prayed—or heard others pray—in a groove that flowed as easily as Jesus talking with his Father?

You might struggle to find the right words when you pray. One of the best ways to find your voice is to pray Scripture—in other words, take the words of the Bible and make them your own. You can start by praying this prayer like you really mean it. Then flip to the Psalms and say them to God. Or you can take any part of the Bible and turn it into a prayer. If it says, "When you talk, do not say harmful things, but say what people need—words that will help others become stronger" (Ephesians 4:29, NCV), just flip it around and say it fresh: "God, I don't want to say harmful things. Help me say what people need—words that will make them stronger."

➡ **WRAP** In this prayer that's so famous it's simply called "The Lord's Prayer," Jesus shows you what prayer can be: It's real. And it's simple. It can be really simple.

》 MORE THOUGHTS TO MULL

- What's easy for you about praying? What makes it tough?

- Why didn't Jesus offer a prayer designed to impress people? How do you think really religious people reacted when they heard Jesus' simple prayer?

- How often do you hear The Lord's Prayer in church? Ask your pastor when and why you use it in your church.

- Pray it: *Father, may your name be honored. May your kingdom come soon. Give me food day by day. And forgive my sins, just as I forgive those who have sinned against me. And don't let me give in to temptation.*

» MORE SCRIPTURES TO DIG

- This isn't the only time Jesus prays in the book of Luke. He spoke to his Father when the heavens split open (**Luke 3:21-22**). He went to desolate places to pray (**Luke 5:16**), and once he went to a mountain to pray for a whole night (**Luke 6:12**). He prayed in private (**Luke 9:18**), but he was unfazed by praying in front of his disciples (**Luke 9:28**). And he prayed before he went to the cross (**Luke 22:41-44**).

- You might wonder whether Luke chopped off the last line of The Lord's Prayer that you say in church. The part that says, "For yours is the kingdom and the power and the glory forever. Amen," shows up only in some later copies of Bible manuscripts, so many Bible translations add it as a footnote. But it's still good stuff.

- Jesus likely taught The Lord's Prayer on many occasions. Peek at **Matthew 6:1-15** to see the version recorded there—along with other wise words on prayer, including warnings against showing off in prayer and babbling endlessly in an attempt to impress God.

7. APPLAUDING GOD

Prayer is praise

Psalm 18:31

For who is God besides the Lord?

And who is the Rock except our God?

➜ **START** Some preachers say that if you yell during football games, then you should cheer for God in church. Then again, at football games girls spit peanut shells and guys paint their chests with their team's colors. But you get the point. The thought of "praising God" might seem sappy or phony. Yet it's the first big part of prayer. If you've got reason to speak highly of God, then you should say it straight to God's face.

When have you ever been so excited that you screamed out loud? Has that feverish excitement ever struck you while you're in church? Why—or why not?

➜ **READ** Psalm 18:25-34

²⁵To the faithful you show yourself faithful, to the blameless you show yourself blameless, ²⁶to the pure you show yourself pure, but to the devious you show yourself shrewd. ²⁷You save the humble but bring low those whose eyes are haughty. ²⁸You, Lord, keep my lamp burning; my God turns my darkness into light. ²⁹With your help I can advance against a troop; with my God I can scale a wall. ³⁰As for God, his way is perfect: The Lord's word is flawless; he shields all who take refuge in him. ³¹For who is God besides the Lord? And who is the Rock except our God? ³²It is God who arms me with strength and keeps my way secure. ³³He makes my feet like the feet of a deer; he causes me to stand on the heights. ³⁴He trains my hands for battle; my arms can bend a bow of bronze.

➜ **THINK** Here's what you've heard so far about prayer: Prayer is about a relationship, not just requests. God invites you to ask. He has a wild desire to meet your needs. God has a huge will he aims to give you. He wants you to ask for the right things for the right reasons. Prayer can be really simple.

Now during the next four studies, we'll peel away the big parts of prayer that you heard about last time—praise, repentance, asking, and yielding. First up: praise—the P in PRAY.

Israel's King David sang Psalm 18 when God spared him from David's biggest enemies. It's easy to see that his applause falls into a couple of categories: Praise for *what God does for him* and praise for *who God is*.

What good things has God done in and for David? List examples.

By the way, David's not talking about your modern compound bow with an easy 45-pound draw. God is going to make him strong enough to bend pipe with his bare hands. Actually, bronze is a vivid way to say "really mighty" because bows were always made of wood. And that "deer" is an animal whose agility lets it walk on skinny ledges in mountainous, rocky terrain.

What all does David praise about God?

➡ **LIVE** So what has God done *for* you? What things—big or little—can you applaud him for? What has he done *in* you—making you better than you could be on your own?

What about God do you find so spectacular that you want to tell him about it?

➡ **WRAP** In the New Testament, Paul quizzed the church in Corinth, "What do you have that God hasn't given you?" (1 Corinthians 4:7, NLT). The answer? Nothing! Everything good in your life is a gift from God, and that means you've got something to praise him for. And because he's the kind of God who gives you good gifts, he's worth praising just because of who he is.

» MORE THOUGHTS TO MULL

- When and how do you praise God?

- What do you like about applauding God? What makes you uncomfortable about it?

- If you wrote a poem or a song or an essay of praise to God, what would you say? Or what would you draw to applaud him? (That's a hint. Try it.)

- Pray it: No ready-made prayer this time. Use your own words to talk to God about what he's done for you—and about who he is.

» MORE SCRIPTURES TO DIG

- The word *praise* comes from a Latin word for "value" or "price." Praising God, then, is declaring his worth. Flip to **Revelation 5:6-14** to see "every creature in heaven and on earth and under the earth and on the sea" break out in spontaneous worship of Jesus, the Lamb. They declare that he deserves every bit of praise they can give him: "Worthy is the Lamb, who was slain, to receive power and wealth and wisdom and strength and honor and glory and praise!"

- The Bible is packed with songs or "psalms" of praise, both in the book of Psalms and elsewhere. **Psalm 100** tells you how and why to praise God. It's short enough to memorize. So is **Psalm 150**, which details a host of energetic ways that God's people worship him, including horns, dancing, and clashing symbols. For more examples, check out **Exodus 15:1-21; 1 Samuel 2:1-10; 1 Chronicles 16:7-36; and Daniel 2:20-23**.

- Real worship isn't forced. If you want to praise more, study God more. Worship shoots forth like an erupting geyser whenever you glimpse God—seeing both what he does and who he is. Check out **Luke 19:37-40** to see who will praise God if you don't.

8. BUSTED

Prayer is repentance

Psalm 51:10

Create in me a pure heart, O God,

and renew a steadfast spirit within me.

➡ **START** Wrap your mind around this Old Testament scene: King David, the greatest-ever ruler of Israel, commits adultery. Nathan, God's spokesperson, shrewdly confronts the king, who has a lot to be sorry for. Not only has he taken Uriah's wife, Bathsheba, as his own, but he's also removed Uriah from the picture permanently by having him killed in battle (2 Samuel 11–12). Repentance—the R in PRAY—isn't just saying you're sorry. It's having a total change of heart about wrongdoing. It's recognizing the sinfulness of an action and deciding you don't want to live that way anymore. David's prayer of repentance is one of the best-known passages of the Bible.

When have you had to 'fess up to something—big or small?

➡ **READ** Psalm 51:1-4, 7, 10

> [1]Have mercy on me, O God, according to your unfailing love; according to your great compassion blot out my transgressions. [2]Wash away all my iniquity and cleanse me from my sin. [3]For I know my transgressions, and my sin is always before me. [4]Against you, you only, have I sinned and done what is evil in your sight; so you are right in your verdict and justified when you judge. [7]Cleanse me with hyssop, and I will be clean; wash me, and I will be whiter than snow. [10]Create in me a pure heart, O God, and renew a steadfast spirit within me.

➡ **THINK** What's the first thing David asks God for? What's he counting on to motivate God's forgiveness?

What does David want God to do about his sin?

In the Old Testament, sacrifices and ritual washing symbolized God's removing sin and pulling people back to him. The New Testament says God does an even more thorough scrubbing up. "He saved us through the washing of rebirth and renewal by the Holy Spirit" (Titus 3:5).

How honest is David about his guilt? How do you know?

David uses three different words for the sin he's been in. *Transgression* is an act of rebellion and disloyalty. *Iniquity* usually means sinning on purpose. And plain old *sin* is an act that misses a command God has made totally clear. David says God's guilty verdict is right. This is a guy who has blown it and knows it.

➔   **LIVE** What sins are worth admitting to God?

Whenever you sin, you put a brick between you and God. If you let sins pile up, you build a wall. God wants you to own up to your sins, whether they feel little or big. By the way, if you believe you're guiltless, then 1 John 1:8 hits you hard: "If we claim to be without sin, we deceive ourselves and the truth is not in us." The next verse, though, tells how to get hold of

God's forgiveness: "If we confess our sins, he is faithful and just and will forgive us our sins and purify us from all unrighteousness" (1 John 1:9).

What prevents you from admitting you've done wrong—and asking God to wipe that sin away?

➔   **WRAP**   You might find it tough to say, "I was wrong." But your relationship with Jesus really begins when you realize you've done wrong—that you need him as your Savior from sin and as your Lord to lead you to new life. Prayer is your chance to come clean.

»   MORE THOUGHTS TO MULL

- How easy is it for you to admit you've done something wrong?

- Suppose no one knows about some sin you've committed. Why confess it?

- What does confessing your faults to people have to do with repentance? When do you need to 'fess up to human beings?

- Pray it: *Have mercy on me, O God, according to your unfailing love. Create in me a pure heart, O God, and renew a steadfast spirit within me.*

»   MORE SCRIPTURES TO DIG

- Read about David's sin in **2 Samuel 11** and his admission of guilt in **2 Samuel 12:1-13**.

- It's not always easy to spot your own wrongdoing. But God will kindly, gently point out your shortcomings if you ask him to keep you honest with yourself. Pray these words from **Psalm 139:23-24**: "Search me, God, and know my heart; test me and know my anxious thoughts. See if there is any offensive way in me, and lead me in the way everlasting."

- If you don't grasp the basics of why Jesus lived and died, you'll find it tough to understand why repentance is a key part of prayer. **Colossians 1:21-23** lays out the facts: "At one time you were separated from God. You were his enemies in your minds, and the evil things you did were against God. But now God has made you his friends again. He did this through Christ's death in the body so that he might bring you into God's presence as people who are holy, with no wrong, and with nothing of which God can judge you guilty. This will happen if you continue strong and sure in your faith. You must not be moved away from the hope brought to you by the Good News that you heard" (NCV). Jesus died for your sins so you could ditch evil, do right, and stick tight to him☐ now and forever.

9. ASK AND RECEIVE

Prayer is asking

Psalm 77:11-12

I will remember the deeds of the Lord; yes, I will remember your miracles of long ago.

I will consider all your works and meditate on all your mighty deeds.

➜   **START** Prayer can seem a bit like plunking your money into a pop machine. Lots of times you get an immediate *kerkerkerplunk... phhhtt...aaah* as you obtain exactly what you wanted. Other times, these tiny words light up: "Please make another selection." And there's that nervous moment between punching a button and getting your soda, when you wonder if the machine ate your money. Well, that's just like waiting for an answer to prayer. Actually, that's where the similarities end. See, you're not dealing with a machine. You're dealing with God.

When have you asked God for something and not gotten what you wanted—right away or ever? How did you feel?

➜   **READ** Psalm 77:1-14

[1]I cried out to God for help; I cried out to God to hear me. [2]When I was in distress, I sought the Lord; at night I stretched out untiring hands, and I would not be comforted. [3]I remembered you, God, and I groaned; I meditated, and my spirit grew faint. [4]You kept my eyes from closing; I was too troubled to speak. [5]I thought about the former days, the years of long ago; [6]I remembered my songs in the night. My heart meditated and my spirit asked: [7]"Will the Lord reject forever? Will he never show his favor again? [8]Has his unfailing love vanished forever? Has his promise failed for all time? [9]Has God forgotten to be merciful? Has he in anger withheld his compassion?" [10]Then I thought, "To this I will appeal: the years when the Most High stretched out his right hand. [11]I will remember the deeds of the Lord; yes, I will remember your miracles of long ago. [12]I will consider all your works and meditate on all your mighty deeds." [13]Your ways, God, are holy. What god is as great as our God? [14]You are the God who performs miracles; you display your power among the peoples.

➔ **THINK** Asking is the A in PRAY—and you'd think it would be the easy part of prayer. Suppose you try hard to figure out the good things God wants for you. But when you put in your prayer request and God doesn't instantly send what you're expecting, then you might start to wonder where he is, maybe even wonder if he still cares for you. But asking isn't just about getting. It's about trusting.

Psalm 77 was written by an Old Testament musician named Asaph (AY-saf). How is Asaph feeling—mind, heart, and body—when he starts to pray?

When God's answer doesn't come right away, what is Asaph wondering about God?

What all does Asaph remember about God? What happens?

Asking all night long doesn't bring Asaph rest. By remembering God's long history of helping Asaph and other people—with deeds that were 100 percent genuine, 100 percent kind—he finally finds hope. Asaph tells God what he wants. Then he decides to wait—and to trust.

➡️   **LIVE** How do you feel when you have to wait for an answer to prayer?

Think of events in your life—big or small—where you can look back and say, "God took care of me." You were sick, and God made you well. You were sad, and God cheered you up. You were really needy, and God met your need. Got any stories like that? Or can you think of some stories like that about your family or friends? What could recalling those things do for you when obvious answers to your prayers don't come right away?

➡️   **WRAP** God is way more than a soda machine. He's your all-knowing, all-loving Father who responds to your requests one by one, all to give you the right gifts at the right time. So don't be surprised when instead of a "yes" you get a "no" or a "not now." Ask and keep on asking, and remember when it's time to trust.

» MORE THOUGHTS TO MULL

- Does Asaph ever figure out where God's long-awaited answer is?

- When have you gotten "no" or "not now" replies from God?

- When have you been challenged to trust God about something huge because you didn't immediately receive the answer you'd hoped for?

- Pray it: *God, help me be bold enough to ask you for everything I need. Help me be patient enough to wait for your best answers.*

» MORE SCRIPTURES TO DIG

- Asaph was a musician appointed by King David to lead worship in the tabernacle, the Old Testament worship center that was used until a temple was built. Several of his songs were picked for inclusion in the Psalms, the hymnbook of ancient Israel. You can read his greatest hits in **Psalms 50** and **73–83**. One favorite: **Psalm 73**, a great read when you're tempted to think God has ditched you.

- **Psalm 31:14-15** are simple verses you can memorize to remind you that God is worth trusting—and that his answers come at the right time: "I trust in you, Lord; I say, 'You are my God.' My times are in your hands."

- Asaph didn't just dig back to the details of his own life to see God's care. He thought back to the big miracles God had pulled off to help his people, the Israelites. He found concrete reasons to trust God, recalling them in **Psalm 77:15-20**. Read the rest of this psalm, and you'll spot God's mighty care. At the end, there's an encouraging conclusion, an awesome picture of God's protection and provision: "You led your people like a flock" (**Psalm 77:20**).

10. GOD'S WILL IS GOD'S BEST

Prayer is yielding

Matthew 26:39

Going a little farther, he fell with his face to the ground and prayed,

"My Father, if it is possible, may this cup be taken from me.

Yet not as I will, but as you will."

➜ **START** Mere hours before his death, Jesus prays desperately in the Garden of Gethsemane, a name that has a startling literal meaning: "the oil press." Facing his Father's plans for him to go to the cross as the sacrificial, sin-absorbing Passover Lamb—a death more awful than any other human will ever face—Jesus questions again and again whether there's another way to save humankind. Despite his anguish, he stays fixed on doing God's will no matter what, and ultimately he yields to his Father's choice. When you're driving, "yielding" means giving someone the right of way. When you're praying, "yielding" means agreeing to God's answer, whatever it might be. It's saying, "God, I want it your way." Yielding is the Y in PRAY.

What's the biggest, most important thing you've ever requested from God—and he gave you an answer you didn't want?

➜ **READ** Matthew 26:36-46

> ³⁶Then Jesus went with his disciples to a place called Gethsemane, and he said to them, "Sit here while I go over there and pray." ³⁷He took Peter and the two sons of Zebedee along with him, and he began to be sorrowful and troubled. ³⁸Then he said to them, "My soul is overwhelmed with sorrow to the point of death. Stay here and keep watch with me."
>
> ³⁹Going a little farther, he fell with his face to the ground and prayed, "My Father, if it is possible, may this cup be taken from me. Yet not as I will, but as you will."
>
> ⁴⁰Then he returned to his disciples and found them sleeping. "Couldn't you men keep watch with me for one hour?" he asked Peter. ⁴¹"Watch and pray so that you will not fall into temptation. The spirit is willing, but the flesh is weak."

⁴²He went away a second time and prayed, "My Father, if it is not possible for this cup to be taken away unless I drink it, may your will be done."

⁴³When he came back, he again found them sleeping, because their eyes were heavy. ⁴⁴So he left them and went away once more and prayed the third time, saying the same thing.

⁴⁵Then he returned to the disciples and said to them, "Are you still sleeping and resting? Look, the hour is near, and the Son of Man is delivered into the hands of sinners. ⁴⁶Rise! Let us go! Here comes my betrayer!"

➔   **THINK** Jot down words and phrases that describe how Jesus feels.

Jesus' anguish is a sorrow so deep it almost kills. He sweats blood (Luke 22:44), an extreme stress reaction called *hematidrosis.*

What does Jesus ask his Father?

Jesus presses his request three times (Matthew 26:39, 42, 44). "This cup" isn't just Christ's physical suffering and death on the cross. As the total sacrifice for our sins, he would suffer the brunt of God's wrath and be cut off from the Father (Matthew 27:46).

When it isn't possible for "this cup to be taken away," what does Jesus want?

➜ **LIVE** Jesus is absolutely set on doing his Father's will, but he still wonders if there's a way out. When have you struggled with God like that? What were you battling about?

Jesus knew why he had to die. But often God's reasons for saying no to us aren't so obvious. How easy or hard is it for you to accept God's will when you don't get what's going on?

How long should you pray for something you really want—something you believe God should really want too?

Jesus shows what it means to ask and keep on asking—and to yield: He asks for "yes" until his Father makes it clear that his answer is "no." And then he agrees to go God's way.

➡   **WRAP** We can pray hard for what we think is right, good, and fair; yet God alone knows the perfect response to every request. Like Jesus, sometimes we struggle to accept this fact: When we get God's will, we get God's best.

»   MORE THOUGHTS TO MULL

- How is yielding to God different from rolling over, giving up, and saying "Okay, God, whatever"?

- This biblical scene shows that prayer can be rough work. How ready are you for sweaty prayer? Explain.

- How do you feel about the anguish Jesus suffered for you as he journeyed to the cross?

- Pray it: *In everything I pray, God, I want your way.*

»   MORE SCRIPTURES TO DIG

- God always gives what's good to those who trust him, but that doesn't mean we always grasp God's reasoning. Whether your request is big or little, it's hard to hear God say no. It's also excruciating to hear people's too-easy explanations for why God, for example, doesn't heal someone you love. Mull this wisdom from the mouth of someone who's been there: In **2 Corinthians 12:7-10** Paul says he prayed three times for God to take away a "thorn," likely an opponent or a serious physical ailment. Paul doesn't get what he wants, yet he receives one amazing thing. He gets enough of God's power to see him through his suffering.

- **2 Samuel 12:15-23** shows Israel's King David wrestling with God for an answer—and yielding at the right time.

- Reread the Garden of Gethsemane scene in **Matthew 26:36-46**. When Jesus counts on his closest friends to pray with him, they snooze, and he's left alone to struggle with his Father. You might face your biggest problems alone. Still, God commands us to stick tight and pray together. (More on that in Study 13.)

11. GRATITUDE NOTED

Prayer is saying thanks

Luke 17:15-16

One of them, when he saw he was healed, came back, praising God in a loud voice.

He threw himself at Jesus' feet and thanked him.

➜   **START** You probably wouldn't stand around looking stupefied and expressionless if a sweepstakes van rolled up to your home and dispensed enough cash for you to live lavishly for the rest of your days on earth. Yet God gives you even more enormous blessings, blanketing you with total care from here to heaven. You don't want to forget to write him a thank-you note. In fact, we all should write him *lots* of thank-you notes.

When has receiving a gift caused you to spout something like "Thankyouthankyouthankyou!"?

➜   **READ** Luke 17:11-19

11Now on his way to Jerusalem, Jesus traveled along the border between Samaria and Galilee. 12As he was going into a village, ten men who had leprosy met him. They stood at a distance 13and called out in a loud voice, "Jesus, Master, have pity on us!"

14When he saw them, he said, "Go, show yourselves to the priests." And as they went, they were cleansed.

15One of them, when he saw he was healed, came back, praising God in a loud voice. 16He threw himself at Jesus' feet and thanked him—and he was a Samaritan.

17Jesus asked, "Were not all ten cleansed? Where are the other nine? 18Was no one found to return and give praise to God except this foreigner?" 19Then he said to him, "Rise and go; your faith has made you well."

➜   **THINK** In the Bible the term *leprosy* could mean a number of skin disorders, but its symptoms typically started with white patches on the skin and ended in disfigurement. Anyone suffering from leprosy was pronounced unclean (Leviticus 13:3), cut off from the community, and judged unfit to worship. Anyone coming in contact with a leprosy victim was also temporarily banned from worship.

These 10 guys boldly call out to Jesus, begging for pity. What do they get when they act on his command?

Only a miraculous, total healing would allow someone suffering from leprosy back into society (Numbers 12:9-15). Jesus sends the men to the priests for an official skin check-up. Not only are they physically healed, but they're also allowed to return to their families and friends.

You can bet none of those guys grumbled at the gift Jesus gave them. Yet only one comes back to thank Jesus. What does Jesus wonder about the others? And what does he say has happened in the one man who said thanks?

Bonus! In verse 14, the leper is "cleansed." But then in verse 19, Jesus uses a bigger, more complete word that means "made well." Besides receiving a physical healing, this guy gets spiritual healing.

➜   **LIVE** What runs through your head when someone gives you an amazing gift? Is it easier to focus on the giver—or the gift? Why?

How do you feel when you say thanks in the right way and at the right time? What does it do for you?

What good things in your life do you want to thank God for right now? Jot some down, then pray.

➜   **WRAP** What can you say after you *praise-repent-ask-yield*? You can thank the One who gives you everything you've got☐ from material possessions and talents, to friends and family, to a home in heaven. It's time to "Enter his gates with thanksgiving and his courts with praise; give thanks to him and praise his name" (Psalm 100:4).

» MORE THOUGHTS TO MULL

- At the time of Jesus, leprosy was believed to be incurable. What do you think those leprosy victims expected Jesus to do for them?

- Where do you think the other nine guys went? Why didn't they come back?

- When have you forgotten to say thanks? How can you make that right?

- Pray it: *Thanks, God, for everything you've given me.*

» MORE SCRIPTURES TO DIG

- In **Leviticus 13:45-46** you get a picture of life with leprosy and other skin diseases: "Anyone with such a defiling disease must wear torn clothes, let their hair be unkempt, cover the lower part of their face and cry out, 'Unclean! Unclean!' As long as they have the disease they remain unclean. They must live alone; they must live outside the camp." Leprosy was a physical condition that caused social and spiritual isolation. As one scholar puts it: "The patient died a social death much sooner and far worse than physical death."

- Religious rules said Jesus should shun victims of leprosy. Yet he touched them (**Mark 1:40-45**), and he commanded his disciples to heal them (**Matthew 10:8**). He made the man in this account a hero.

- Looking for tips on saying thanks? **1 Thessalonians 5:18** says when to give thanks: "Give thanks in all circumstances; for this is God's will for you in Christ Jesus." **Psalm 136** piles up reason after reason to be grateful. **Psalm 107:8-9** sums up the best reasons to be thankful: "Let them give thanks to the Lord for his unfailing love and his wonderful deeds for humankind, for he satisfies the thirsty and fills the hungry with good things."

12. BREATHE EASY

Making time to pray

Mark 1:35

Very early in the morning, while it was still dark,

Jesus got up, left the house and went off to a solitary place, where he prayed.

→ **START** Whether you know it or not, your body does three kinds of breathing. There's the type of breathing you do all the time—short, automatic bursts. Or you might breathe for others—like in mouth-to-mouth emergencies. Then there's the breathing you have to think about—like when you're doing your utmost to run at a blazing pace. Well, prayer is like breathing. You can breathe prayers nonstop, talking to God wherever you go and whatever you do. There are major, panicked prayers that you say for others. And some prayers you need to think about, setting aside time just to focus on talking with God. It's a spiritual workout that causes steady growth, but it's easy to shove aside.

Just like you do three kinds of breathing, you can fill your life with three kinds of prayer. So which kind comes easiest for you? Which would you like to learn to do better?

→ **READ** Mark 1:32-35

[32]That evening after sunset the people brought to Jesus all the sick and demon-possessed. [33]The whole town gathered at the door, [34]and Jesus healed many who had various diseases. He also drove out many demons, but he would not let the demons speak because they knew who he was.

[35]Very early in the morning, while it was still dark, Jesus got up, left the house and went off to a solitary place, where he prayed.

→ **THINK** A few quick verses in Mark 1:21-37 recap a couple of days in the life of Jesus. He starts off by teaching in a synagogue, a local center of Jewish worship and teaching. He tosses out a demon, heals the mother-in-law of one of his followers, and then drives away a bunch more demons and heals a bunch more people. But the next morning, instead of sleeping late, he heads out to pray.

When exactly does Jesus get up? Where does he go?

The phrase *very early* literally means "very much at night." Jesus was starting his job of preaching from town to town. He seeks the strength that only time spent talking with his Father can provide.

➜   **LIVE** How much has prayer become a habit in your life? Details, please.

What people, places, things, or activities get in the way of your praying?

When and where could you set aside some focused time to pray?

Your life is more about making grades than doing miracles. But how could making time to pray help your days?

What does prayer have to do with your "ministry," whatever that is-volunteering at school, serving through church, or just doing your home-work and helping around the house?

➔ **WRAP** Do you ever feel too busy to pray? Look at Jesus' day and ponder this: When you think there's no time to pray, that's when you need prayer the most.

» MORE THOUGHTS TO MULL

- Who do you know that seems to have built a healthy and happy habit of prayer? Ask them how they found their stride.

- Have you ever worried about getting over-the-top spiritual—as in, praying too much? Explain your answer.

- Suppose you wanted to do a powerful prayer workout each day. How could you start slow? What would you pray about?

- Pray it: *God, I'm starting to learn what prayer can do. Show me how to make it a priority.*

» MORE SCRIPTURES TO DIG

- Jesus came to destroy the power of the Devil (**1 John 3:8**), including the Devil's horde of "demons," the kind of evil, supernatural spirits you see in this passage. Jesus probably silenced the demons in **Mark 1:34** so he could reveal who he is in his own time and in his own way. Jesus wants to be known as more than the preacher who makes demons shriek. Many other places in the New Testament illustrate the fact that the healings and demon tossings he did that day weren't one-of-a-kind events. Jesus and his followers healed many people and drove out many demons.

- Check out what **Luke 5:16, 6:12,** and **9:18** say about Jesus getting away to pray.

- Read the whole passage of **Mark 1:21-37** to catch some intriguing points about Jesus. People are "amazed" (Mark 1:22) because Jesus doesn't have to quote other authorities to support what he says, unlike the religious scholars (the "teachers of the law"). *Amazed* is a strong word, like getting smacked upside the head. Then a demon figures out exactly who Jesus is—"the Holy One of God" (Mark 1:24). People are wowed once again, but this time their amazement is tinged with alarm. They'd never seen anything like this. News about Jesus spreads rapidly.

13. GRAB ANOTHER HAND

Praying with friends

Matthew 18:19

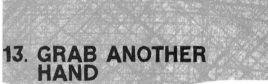

"Again, truly I tell you that if two of you on earth agree about anything you ask for,

it will be done for you by my Father in heaven."

➜   **START** Maybe you bust a sweat the instant anyone says, "Let's pray." When it's time for group prayer, you shut your eyes and clench your jaw, all the while feeling the scorching glances of everyone who's peeking to see why you're not praying. Actually, you don't really know if they're staring at you. They might feel equally queasy. So look at these biblical reasons why praying with friends is good, and try to think of praying with others as a "get to" instead of a "have to."

How much do you like praying with other people? Is it wildly agreeable— or highly uncomfortable?

➜   **READ** Matthew 18:19-20

Jesus said: [19]"Again, truly I tell you that if two of you on earth agree about anything you ask for, it will be done for you by my Father in heaven. [20]For where two or three come together in my name, there am I with them."

➜   **THINK** What does Jesus promise will happen if you and a friend or two "agree about anything you ask for"? What exactly does he mean by that?

What's not to like about that promise? It sounds like you just have to round up some pals, get in sync on what to ask, state your requests, and wait for all sorts of good stuff to drop from heaven! Before you make that powerful verse your one-and-only prayer motto, think how it fits in with the Bible's whole message on prayer. If you recall 1 John 5:14 ("This is the confidence we have in approaching God: that if we ask anything according to his will, he hears us"), then you realize that you and your friends still need to ask for what *God* wants.

Jesus makes another promise about what occurs when people get together in his name. What's his second good reason to pray with others?

➜ **LIVE** Does praying with people make talking to God easier or harder for you? Why?

Say it in your own words: What are the benefits you miss out on if you don't pray with others?

Brainstorm: What sorts of things can you pray for with your friends?

Check out these examples from the early church: Believers prayed together a lot (Acts 1:14). They prayed together because it was a top priority (Acts 2:42). They prayed together for guidance (Acts 1:24). They prayed together that they would be filled by God's Spirit (Acts 4:29-31). They prayed together at the beach (Acts 21:5). They prayed together in prison (Acts 16:25). They prayed together for persecuted believers (Acts 12:5). They prayed together when they faced a crisis—like a shipwreck (Acts 27:27-29). And they prayed together to launch people into ministry (Acts 13:1-3). Get it? They prayed together about *everything*.

Jot down the names of some people with whom you wouldn't be deathly afraid to pray. What's your plan to make praying together happen?

➜   **WRAP** Even if you don't grab hands, praying together is still a holy way to glue your hearts to each other and to God. Jesus promises a one-of-a-kind experience of his presence when you link up in prayer. And it gives power to what you ask.

》   MORE THOUGHTS TO MULL

- Think deep: From what you see in all of those brief Bible passages from the book of Acts, why was praying together important to the early Christians?

- Get specific: When has praying with others felt awful? When has it been good?

- Does being shy about praying in front of others make you an awful Christian? Explain.

- If you could change one thing about praying with others to make it easier, what would it be?

- How do you react to all of the praying that goes on in an average church service—or maybe a Christian school chapel? Is your brain engaged in that group prayer—or not? If not, what can you do to truly join in?

- Pray it: Grab a friend and talk to God.

» MORE SCRIPTURES TO DIG

- To see how prayer fits into the whole story, check out the passages surrounding any of those accounts of group prayer in the book of Acts.

- You might wonder if Christian friends are an optional add-on to your faith in Jesus. Actually, they're how you survive and thrive. **2 Timothy 2:22** says what Christian friends can do for you: Together with them you can, "Flee the evil desires of youth and pursue righteousness, faith, love and peace, along with those who call on the Lord out of a pure heart." Having someone to "call on the Lord" with is what praying with others is all about.

14. LOUD AND PROUD

Bad Bible prayers, part 1

Luke 18:13

But the tax collector stood at a distance. He would not even look up to heaven,

but beat his breast and said, "God, have mercy on me, a sinner."

➜ **START** When Pastor Gruntseth prays, he shouts. He grabs the pulpit so it shakes. He sounds as if he's wired straight to the Holy Ghost. And everyone loves to hear him pray. Uh, well, maybe everyone except God.

Of all the people you know, who would you vote most likely to win a gold medal in an Olympics of prayer? Why do you think that?

➜ **READ** Luke 18:10-14

Jesus said: [10]"Two men went up to the temple to pray, one a Pharisee and the other a tax collector. [11]The Pharisee stood by himself and prayed: 'God, I thank you that I am not like other people—robbers, evildoers, adulterers—or even like this tax collector. [12]I fast twice a week and give a tenth of all I get.'

[13]"But the tax collector stood at a distance. He would not even look up to heaven, but beat his breast and said, 'God, have mercy on me, a sinner.'

[14]"I tell you that this man, rather than the other, went home justified before God. For all those who exalt themselves will be humbled, and those who humble themselves will be exalted."

➜ **THINK** Back in Bible times, most people would have said tax collectors had plenty to be sorry for. First of all, they worked for the Romans☐ the hated occupiers of Israel. Not only that, but when they collected the government's due, they always helped themselves to a heap off the top. Pharisees were religious leaders known for keeping rules, doing everything right—and making sure everyone saw their acts of goodness.

In this story from Jesus, two guys pray. What's the difference in how they talk to God?

How does God score the two pray-ers? Which one has God's favor—the one who brags that he always does right, or the one who admits he's been really wrong?

Here's what God is looking for when you pray: Psalm 51:17 says "God, you will not reject a heart that is broken and sorry for sin" (NCV). And Psalm 101:5 says "I will not allow people to be proud and look down on others" (NCV). The Pharisee thought his spiritual activities and eloquent words would score bonus points with God. But Jesus says it was the tax collector who truly met God through his prayer.

➔ **LIVE** Jesus said, "And when you pray, do not be like the hypocrites, for they love to pray standing in the synagogues and on the street corners to be seen by others" (Matthew 6:5). Say it in your own words: What makes prayer in front of others wrong?

Would God have liked the tax collector's prayer even better if he'd prayed longer? Explain.

Jesus sometimes prayed all night (Luke 6:12), but he also criticized prayers that kept going...and going...and going...that is, if they kept going for the wrong reasons: "And when you pray, do not keep on babbling like pagans, for they think they will be heard because of their many words" (Matthew 6:7).

How would you describe the kinds of prayers God likes to hear?

➡   **WRAP** God deserves your utmost respect. Yet your prayers don't have to be loud, long, or lovely to connect with him. Remember, you're talking to your Father (Matthew 6:9). In fact, you're talking to your Friend (John 15:15).

» MORE THOUGHTS TO MULL

- Does Jesus' story mean prayer should never be beautiful, songlike, heartfelt, or heated? Why—or why not?

- Have you ever prayed to impress God? What did you say? How did you say it?

- When you pray with other people, how do you keep prayer from becoming a contest?

- Pray it: *God, help me to just talk to you☐ to tell you what's going on in my head and my heart.*

» MORE SCRIPTURES TO DIG

- Jesus doesn't stop at teaching his early followers how to pray. He tells them how *not* to pray, banning prayers that are proud—or public for the wrong reasons. Read **Matthew 6:5-13** and check out how this Bible passage leads into the simple prayer Jesus taught us to pray.

- Jesus didn't mean you should never pray in front of other people. After all, Jesus did it (**Luke 3:21**; **John 17:1-26**), and you've already learned that group prayer is a great way to talk to God (**Matthew 18:20**). But the Bible seems to show Jesus praying in private way more than in public. He wants to deflate people who pump up their religion in front of others just so they can be seen or heard.

- Check out **1 Kings 18:16-40**, where the prophet Elijah mocks the followers of the fake god Baal for praying loud and long. When their god didn't hear them, they "shouted louder and slashed themselves with swords and spears, as was their custom, until their blood flowed" (1 Kings 18:28).

15. FIRST THINGS FIRST

Bad Bible prayers, part 2

Matthew 5:23-24

"Therefore, if you are offering your gift at the altar

and there remember that your brother or sister has something against you,

leave your gift there in front of the altar.

First go and be reconciled to that person; then come and offer your gift."

➜   **START** You know how it goes when you clash with a friend. Your conversations limp. You quit texting. At every turn you avoid each other. When you do stumble into a face-to-face meeting with each other, you stammer for words—or you explode. If you ever become out-and-out enemies, your communication quits altogether. You might not realize, however, that your troubles with people can get in the way of your talking with God—and in a big way.

Think back to a spat with a friend. What all happened to your communication? How did you get it going again?

➜   **READ** Matthew 5:21-24

Jesus said: [21]"You have heard that it was said to the people long ago, 'You shall not murder, and anyone who murders will be subject to judgment.' [22]But I tell you that anyone who is angry with a brother or sister will be subject to judgment. Again, anyone who says to a brother or sister, 'Raca,' is answerable to the Sanhedrin. And anyone who says, 'You fool!' will be in danger of the fire of hell. [23]Therefore, if you are offering your gift at the altar and there remember that your brother or sister has something against you, [24]leave your gift there in front of the altar. First go and be reconciled to that person; then come and offer your gift."

➜   **THINK** Jesus starts out talking about a big wrong. Anyone who commits murder, he says, will be "subject to judgment," brought to trial either before God or a human council. Everyone listening to Jesus would know that the Old Testament punishment for murder was hefty—death, generally. What Jesus said next was the real surprise.

That same punishment applies to people who do what? Spot three things.

Raca means "imbecile" or "blockhead." *Fool* has that same meaning, plus it implies more than a bit of wickedness.

Here's the point about prayer: Jesus pictures someone in the solemn inner court of the temple worshiping God. What does Jesus say that person should do before he or she approaches God?

That person who's getting close to God apparently made someone mad and needs to make it right. But the command cuts both ways. If someone has wronged you and you stay bitter toward them, then that bitterness also keeps *you* from getting close to God. Mark 11:25-26 says, "When you stand praying, if you hold anything against anyone, forgive them, so that your Father in heaven may forgive you your sins."

➜   **LIVE** Why do you suppose Jesus puts being angry with other people on a par with murder?

Jesus is speaking in hyped-up language. Yet rage and cruelty are at the heart of murder. So if you're "only" hanging on to anger toward a person or treating someone badly, then you also need God's help. Just because you haven't bumped someone off, that doesn't mean you're a totally mature follower of God.

Why would it bother God if you were having a fight with someone? What business is it of his?

God is the one who defines right and wrong and who commands you to love. So when you lash out at people, you sin against God. The Bible also says that your treatment of people reveals your real attitude toward God: "If we say we love God yet hate a brother or sister, we are liars. For if we do not love a fellow believer, whom we have seen, we cannot love God, whom we have not seen" (1 John 4:20).

➡   **WRAP** The fact that God doesn't tolerate sin might make you a tad afraid to pray. But he tells us what to do. He wants us to clean up our messes. And he wants us to never stop grabbing hold of his forgiveness (1 John 1:8-9).

»   MORE THOUGHTS TO MULL

- If anger and put-downs get in the way of our connecting with God, what other attitudes and behaviors might also be problems we need to clean up?

- Look around your life: What bad relationships with people might be getting in the way of your relationship with God?

- When have you fought with a friend but then put your friendship back together so you got along better than ever?

- Pray it: *God, I want to be right with people so nothing gets in the way of talking to you.*

» MORE SCRIPTURES TO DIG

- If you ponder life for any longer than a minute, you'll soon figure out that we all have plenty of reasons to shrink before God. The Bible says, "For everyone has sinned; we all fall short of God's glorious standard" (**Romans 3:23, NLT**). You can't ignore Bible passages that remind us that God is totally holy—and that we are not. But along with that bad news, keep reading the Bible's best news: Because Jesus paid for your sins by dying on the cross, you can run boldly into God's presence (**Hebrews 10:19-23**). And because of Jesus, you have a new home: "For he has rescued us from the dominion of darkness and brought us into the kingdom of the Son he loves, in whom we have redemption, the forgiveness of sins" (**Colossians 1:13-14**).

- Jesus quotes the Old Testament prophet Isaiah (**Isaiah 29:13**) when he says, " 'These people honor me with their lips, but their hearts are far from me. They worship me in vain' " (**Matthew 15:8-9**). He's talking about people who make up their own religious rules, but his point refers to us too (for instance, whenever we pray to God with our lips but don't honor him with our lives).

16. NO WORRIES

Handing God your troubles

Psalm 5:2

Hear my cry for help,

my King and my God,

for to you I pray.

➜ **START** As Morgan sat at her desk, her head felt near bursting. She had normal issues—such as juggling homework, auditioning for the flute part in a band ensemble, and solving a spat with her best friend. She was sweating the small stuff—like getting on the bus after school—before it drives off without her...again. Then there was a major family crisis looming—her grandpa's recent cancer diagnosis. When Morgan thought about praying, she didn't know where to start. Big, little, in-between— she wasn't sure what God cared about.

How do you cope when life hurls stuff at you?

➜ **READ** Psalm 5:1-8

[1]Listen to my words, Lord, consider my lament. [2]Hear my cry for help, my King and my God, for to you I pray. [3]In the morning, Lord, you hear my voice; in the morning I lay my requests before you and wait expectantly. [4]For you are not a God who is pleased with wickedness; with you, evil people are not welcome. [5]The arrogant cannot stand in your presence. You hate all who do wrong; [6]you destroy those who tell lies. The bloodthirsty and deceitful you, Lord, detest. [7]But I, by your great love, can come into your house; in reverence I bow down toward your holy temple. [8]Lead me, Lord, in your righteousness because of my enemies—make your way straight before me.

➜ **THINK** King David's up early to pray. What does he want God to hear?

Why do you suppose David launches into a lecture on God's dislike of evil?

What does David want God to do to his enemies? Do you think it's okay to pray that way? Why—or why not?

Maybe you've asked God to take revenge on people who cause you problems. Lots of the prayers of the Bible—especially the Psalms—say they want God to do something about evil and evildoers. It's a fair prayer. But notice that David trusts God to do the punishing.

➔   **LIVE** David is a powerful king, a cunning warrior. Why would someone like that need to pray about his troubles?

Philippians 4:6-7 tells you what to do, no matter what wallops you, no matter who you are: "Do not be anxious about anything, but in every situation, by prayer and petition, with thanksgiving, present your requests to God. And the peace of God, which transcends all understanding, will guard your hearts and your minds in Christ Jesus."

What—or who—is the biggest worry in your life right now?

What would you like to tell God about the stuff that causes you to wake up feeling nervous?

➡   **WRAP** The grit of everyday life can grind you down. From front to back, the Bible makes clear God's promise to care. You can "give all your worries and cares to God, for he cares about you" (1 Peter 5:7, NLT). And God doesn't want you to lay just *some* of your cares on him, but all of them.

» MORE THOUGHTS TO MULL

- When do you go to God with your worries—when they first hit or when you run out of other options?

- What small thing bothers you greatly but you don't think you should bug God about it?

- You have the privilege of running to God with your worries, but that doesn't mean you don't need people. Who can help you carry the loads of life?

- Pray it: Tell God about something that's bugging you.

» MORE SCRIPTURES TO DIG

- In Study 3 you learned that God has your every need covered: "So do not worry, saying, 'What shall we eat?' or 'What shall we drink?' or 'What shall we wear?' For the pagans run after all these things, and your heavenly Father knows that you need them" (**Matthew 6:31-32**). Flip to **Matthew 6:25-34** to see everything Jesus says about worry.

- We don't have the power to fix many of the things we fret about. Here's what Jesus says in **Luke 12:25-26**: "Who of you by worrying can add a single hour to your life? Since you cannot do this very little thing, why do you worry about the rest?"

- Jesus wants to help you lift every burden of life. Listen to his promise in **Matthew 11:28-30**: "Come to me, all you who are weary and burdened, and I will give you rest. Take my yoke upon you and learn from me, for I am gentle and humble in heart, and you will find rest for your souls. For my yoke is easy and my burden is light."

- Look at this encouragement to trust in God: "Trust in the Lord forever, for the Lord, the Lord, is the Rock eternal" (**Isaiah 26:4**). And check out these amazing results of leaning on him: "When I said, 'My foot is slipping,' your unfailing love, Lord, supported me. When anxiety was great within me, your consolation brought me joy." That's **Psalm 94:18-19**.

17. DECISIONS, DECISIONS

Getting God's guidance

James 1:5

If any of you lacks wisdom, you should ask God,

who gives generously to all without finding fault,

and it will be given to you.

➜   **START** You maybe remember from Study 4 that God has an *ultimate* will for you—that you be a Christian. A *universal* will—that you heed all those commands God makes clear for everyone. And a *specific* will—that you discover the one-of-a-kind plan he has for you. God makes his ultimate will and universal will blazingly clear in the Bible. But if you want to discover his specific will in the nitty-gritty choices of life, you start by asking him for wisdom.

What's the biggest decision you face in the next year? How will you make your choice?

➜   **READ** James 1:5-8

> ⁵If any of you lacks wisdom, you should ask God, who gives generously to all without finding fault, and it will be given to you. ⁶But when you ask, you must believe and not doubt, because the one who doubts is like a wave of the sea, blown and tossed by the wind. ⁷Those who doubt should not think they will receive anything from the Lord; ⁸they are double-minded and unstable in all they do.

➜   **THINK** Suppose you turn to God for help with knowing where to head in life. What's his attitude as he shares his wise guidance?

Remember? You've got a God who knows exactly what you're facing. He gives wisdom "generously" and "without finding fault." Translation: He's happy to guide you. And he won't make you feel stupid.

According to James, who *won't* receive guidance from God? What are those people like? List some descriptions.

God wants to give wisdom to people who are listening. In Bible terms *listening* means being ready to obey. But being "double-minded" means half of your brain is saying, "I want God's guidance!" and the other half says, "I want to do my own thing!" Your goal is to expect God to give you guidance—and even before you know what that guidance is, tell God you'll obey him.

➜ **LIVE** Think of that whopper decision that's looming over you. If you're going to figure out what to do, what kind of specific wisdom do you need from God?

God's wisdom isn't just for massive choices, but it's for every itty bit of your life. What are some small ways you need God's insight?

When you ask God for wisdom, how do you figure he'll give you an answer and guide you?

That's a huge topic. Here's the quickie answer: God will direct you through the Bible, through circumstances, and through the wise advice of other people. But the process starts with *prayer*. Lay out your needs, and God will figure out how to light your way.

Do you buy the idea that the God of the universe is eager to help you navigate your life—and that it's worth asking for his wisdom? Why—or why not?

➜   **WRAP** Often the biggest thing you need from God isn't a thing at all. It's his wise guidance. When you ask, you won't get wisecracks from God. You'll get wisdom.

≫   MORE THOUGHTS TO MULL

- You can't expect God to drop wisdom on you if you ignore his really clear commands—his universal will. Can you think of any of God's expectations that you're blatantly ignoring?

- Wisdom seldom pops into your brain out of nowhere. Often it comes through people who know God well and who also under-stand the wackiness of life. Like it says in Proverbs 15:22, "Plans fail for lack of counsel, but with many advisers they succeed." So whom do you know who's wise? How can they help you make smart choices?

- Psalm 119:105 says, "Your word is a lamp to my feet and a light for my path." How can you use the Bible to let God speak to you about his plan for your life—his ultimate, universal, and specific will?

- Pray it: Talk to God about some areas where you need guidance, now or down the road.

» MORE SCRIPTURES TO DIG

- Give this whole section a read, **James 1:2-8**. The wisdom in this passage is about more than picking which pair of jeans to wear. It comes on the heels of a section about facing trials. A "trial" is anything that puts you to the test—either from the outside, like persecution, or from inside, like temptation. Trials build "perseverance," the ability to stand firm, like staying on your feet in a storm. They make you "mature and complete," attaining all the coolness God plans for you. So this whole passage assumes you're stuck in a tight spot of life. You need wisdom to get through this brutal-but-beneficial experience. And God is eager to help.

- God's wisdom is more colossal than anything you possess. If you're looking for wisdom, there's no better place to go than to the Totally Wise One. Look at **Proverbs 3:5-7**: "Trust in the Lord with all your heart and lean not on your own understanding; in all your ways submit to him, and he will make your paths straight. Do not be wise in your own eyes; fear the Lord and shun evil." You're less-than-bright if you don't grab every insight you can get from God.

- **James 4:13-16** warns against thinking you know so much that you don't need God. And **Psalm 32:8-9** puts those words in a picture: "I will instruct you and teach you in the way you should go; I will counsel you with my loving eye on you. Do not be like the horse or the mule, which have no understanding but must be controlled by bit and bridle or they will not come to you."

18. THINK BIG

Praying for major stuff

1 Timothy 2:1-2

I urge, then, first of all, that petitions, prayers, intercession and thanksgiving be made for everyone—

for kings and all those in authority,

that we may live peaceful and quiet lives in all godliness and holiness.

➜ **START** Maybe you've never even considered praying for the president. Or for the principal of your school. Perhaps you've never talked to God about AIDS in Africa, world hunger, or global warming. It might feel like a giant step to pray for people on the other side of the world, classmates you barely know, or enemies you know all too well. But God wants to boost these topics to the top of your prayer list.

It's relatively easy to pray for things you want or people you know. What do you think about enlarging the reach of the people, places, and problems you pray for?

➜ **READ** 1 Timothy 2:1-6

> [1]I urge, then, first of all, that petitions, prayers, intercession and thanksgiving be made for everyone—[2]for kings and all those in authority, that we may live peaceful and quiet lives in all godliness and holiness. [3]This is good, and pleases God our Savior, [4]who wants all people to be saved and to come to a knowledge of the truth. [5]For there is one God and one mediator between God and human beings, Christ Jesus, himself human, [6]who gave himself as a ransom for all people.

➜ **THINK** It's hard to spot, but the big topic here is group worship. The apostle Paul is arguing that prayer should be high on the list of things we do at Christian gatherings—especially prayer for people in authority. The point isn't to keep you from talking to God about your personal problems, but to urge you to also pray for those whose actions and decisions impact everyone. It takes all of us to wrap our prayers around them.

Paul starts by rattling off four varieties of prayer. What are they?

Request is telling God your needs and desires. *Prayer* is the broadest word, meaning talking to God either in public or private. The particular Greek word used here for *intercession* implies that prayer should be a conversation with God—it's that idea that you can boldly get close to God. And *thanksgiving* reminds you to show gratitude for what God has already done for you.

That's a lot of prayer. Prayer for whom?

"Everyone" sounds mighty broad, but Paul especially highlights praying for people in authority. You might not have a king in your life, but it's likely you've got a president or a prime minister, a pastor, a principal, and a teacher or two.

Why pray for people in authority? What can prayer accomplish for people who don't know God?

➜   **LIVE** Who in your life qualifies as an "everyone" that you're to pray for? What kind of stuff would be helpful to them? What can you ask God to give them?

Name two or three authorities in your life. What could you pray for them?

➜　　**WRAP** God wants his love to reach around the world. Every person and place on the planet needs his help. Every human needs to know him. And people in authority can help or hinder his plan. These are enormous issues, but not so big that you can't make a difference through prayer.

》　MORE THOUGHTS TO MULL

- Think of a friend who's clueless about God. What would knowing God do for her or him? Is that worth taking the time to pray about it?

- At the time Paul wrote this letter, the head of the Roman Empire was the brutal Emperor Nero. Considering the fact that Nero later killed Paul, he's calling for some money-where-your-mouth-is prayer for people you don't like. Are there any authority figures in your life whom you dislike? Those people need your prayers.

- Pray it: Pray that the authorities in your life would lead well—and that they would help your life, not harm it.

》　MORE SCRIPTURES TO DIG

- The New Testament highlights a couple more categories of big-picture prayers. If you think praying for authorities sounds extreme, look in **Matthew 5:43-44** to spy what Jesus says about praying for your enemies. **Matthew 9:38** coaches us to pray boldly that nonbelievers will come to know him. **Ephesians 6:18-20** starts by encouraging prayer for "all the saints," that is, all followers of Jesus. Then it shifts to prayer for the spread of the Good News about Jesus. **Colossians 4:2-6** and **2 Thessalonians 3:1-2** invite the same brand of world-shaking prayer.

- **Ephesians 3:16-21** is a stunning prayer for more of God. Pray it for yourself, your friends, and your world: "I pray that out of his glorious riches he may strengthen you with power through his Spirit in your inner being, so that Christ may dwell in your hearts through faith. And I pray that you, being rooted and established in love, may have power, together with all the Lord's people, to grasp how wide and long and high and deep is the love of Christ, and to know this love that surpasses knowledge—that you may be filled to the measure of all the fullness of God. Now to him who is able to do immeasurably more than all we ask or imagine, according to his power that is at work within us, to him be glory in the church and in Christ Jesus throughout all generations, for ever and ever! Amen."

19. NO WORDS

Being quiet with God

Job 40:4

"I am unworthy—how can I reply to you?

I put my hand over my mouth."

➔ **START** The Bible showcases plenty of ways to pray. King David—after he'd sinned—crawled back to God on his belly. When Asaph hurt, he wailed. The great Old Testament leader Moses even talked back to God, though he did so with a healthy dose of respect. You can praise, repent, ask, and yield. But there's one more way to pray. Sometimes it's best not to say anything.

Why might you want to be silent before God?

➔ **READ** Job 40:1-9

¹The Lord said to Job: ²"Will the one who contends with the Almighty correct him? Let him who accuses God answer him!"

³Then Job answered the Lord: ⁴"I am unworthy—how can I reply to you? I put my hand over my mouth. ⁵I spoke once, but I have no answer—twice, but I will say no more."

⁶Then the Lord spoke to Job out of the storm: ⁷"Prepare to defend yourself; I will question you, and you shall answer me. ⁸Would you discredit my justice? Would you condemn me to justify yourself? ⁹Do you have an arm like God's, and can your voice thunder like his?"

➔ **THINK** The book of Job—rhymes with *robe,* not *rob*—is almost in the middle of the Bible. On a historical timeline, however, its story falls far earlier. Job is an early Bible guy. He's well-off with a nice home and family. But when disaster strikes, Job gets so mad that he protests a little too loudly about how good he is. God puts an end to Job's spewing. He quiets him down and tells him to listen up.

For the last couple of chapters, Job has listened to God's correction. How does Job feel now? What does he say he'll do?

When Job says he's "unworthy," a more accurate meaning is "I'm small" or "I'm insignificant." He also mumbles something like "I'll shut up now. Really."

➜ **LIVE** Prayer is all about us talking to God about everything that's going on in our hearts and our heads. But remember: Prayer is about a relationship. So it's not talking *at* God. It's talking *with* him.

Have you ever tried to let God speak when you pray? What happened—or why is that a crazy idea?

Even if you want to let God talk, you might not have any idea of how that happens. How does that work? How do you think God could speak to you when you pray?

Don't expect God to talk out loud like he did to Job. If he does, let the rest of us know so we can get a good listen. But the Bible does mention what lots of Christians refer to as God's "still small voice" (1 Kings 19:12, KJV). You might find that the Holy Spirit can give your heart a strong conviction or pop a good thought into your head. He also speaks when you open the Bible and hear him talk in the clearest words possible.

Have you ever sensed God trying to tell you something when you were praying? What point was he trying to make?

➡   **WRAP** You won't hear God if you don't let him get a word in edgewise. If you want to hear him better, then let down your defenses—any attempts to tell God what he should do. Put away distractions—anything that shifts your focus off of God. Take your time—or else you're pushing him out of the conversation. Ask God what he wants to teach you today—or you end up treating him like he's the pizza delivery guy.

» MORE THOUGHTS TO MULL

- Does not saying anything to God really count as prayer? Why—or why not?

- Job shuts up because he realizes his prayers have gotten out of hand. Why else might you choose to spend time being quiet with God?

- Have you ever crossed the line from praying boldly to talking as though you know better than God does?

- Pray it: *God, you are great. Help me to be quiet with you.*

» MORE SCRIPTURES TO DIG

- It's one thing to pour your heart out in prayer. It's another to think you're the only one in the conversation who has something to say.

Sometimes the secret of prayer is to rest in quiet awe. Like **Psalm 46:10** says, "Be still, and know that I am God."

- **Isaiah 30:21** says that at times believers will "hear a voice behind you saying, 'This is the right way. You should go this way' " (NCV).

- Read about that "still small voice" (KJV) or "gentle whisper" (TNIV) in **1 Kings 19:12**. The rest of chapter 19 fills out the scene, where Elijah wails to God that he is fighting evil all alone. Once this great prophet shuts up, God talks to him with words of deep comfort.

- **Exodus 3:1-14** shows Moses' debate with God. Moses removes his shoes and covers his face as a sign of respect, but he still freely disagrees with God. Yet when Moses protests that he's not capable of doing what God commands, God promises to give Moses all the power he needs.

- You can read **Job 42:10-17** to see that at the end of this story, Job dies old and happy, getting back even more than he lost. In the meantime, Job got humble and listened up.

20. TRUST THIS GUY

You can count on Jesus

Luke 8:24

The disciples went and woke him, saying, "Master, Master, we're going to drown!"

He got up and rebuked the wind and the raging waters; the storm subsided, and all was calm.

➜ **START** Leaning over the rail sounds like a good idea—until the boat lurches on a wave and punches your stomach like a Heimlich maneuver. Everything you've eaten in the last month feels like it's just an inch away from becoming fish bait. As the boat keeps rocking...rolling...heaving...dropping...you wish the skipper would head back to shore. With a hearty chuckle, he keeps casting for fish.

You're just sailing through life when out of the blue, you're caught in a storm that will make you sick—or even sink you. What do you expect God will do for you?

➜ **READ** Luke 8:22-25

²²One day Jesus said to his disciples, "Let us go over to the other side of the lake." So they got into a boat and set out. ²³As they sailed, he fell asleep. A squall came down on the lake, so that the boat was being swamped, and they were in great danger.

²⁴The disciples went and woke him, saying, "Master, Master, we're going to drown!"

He got up and rebuked the wind and the raging waters; the storm subsided, and all was calm. ²⁵"Where is your faith?" he asked his disciples.

In fear and amazement they asked one another, "Who is this? He commands even the winds and the water, and they obey him."

➜ **THINK** This scene takes place on the Sea of Galilee, a lake surrounded by steep mountains with narrow valleys. Winds blow toward the lake, whipping up sudden storms that are severe enough to terrify even the professional fishermen among Jesus' followers.

Why would Jesus snooze when his guys are about to die?

When the disciples wake up Jesus, what do you think they expect from him? How sure are they that Jesus can save them?

Three times this passage mentions the wind, emphasizing the severity of the squall. Those fisher-guys can spot danger in the water and the weather. What they can't see is their Master's power.

Jesus instantly calms the storm. So how do the disciples react?

Jesus knows his disciples don't fully comprehend who he is. You can't miss their uncertainty in the question, "Who is this?"

➜   **LIVE** How sure are you that God cares for you, wants to help you, and is worth praying to?

If you said something like "really sure," that's great. If you responded "not so sure," you're normal. So how can you grow in your trust for God—and your readiness to rely on him through prayer?

When you get to know God, you can trust him deep down. When you trust him deep down, you're quick to speak up in prayer. Don't miss the fact that even Jesus' closest followers took time to learn who he was. Jesus notices their lack of faith, but he doesn't mock them for it. He calmly meets their need and saves them from drowning. Then he invites them to believe in him.

➡   **WRAP** God is worth trusting. Rely on him fully. Run to him quickly. Pray to him always.

》 MORE THOUGHTS TO MULL

- What do you know about God that makes him easy to trust? What doubts make it tough to rely on him?

- What do you think convinced the disciples that Jesus is worth trusting?

- Now that you've finished reading *Pray*, what do you plan to do to keep learning how to pray?

- Pray it: *God, help me trust you more and more each day. And help that trust energize my prayers.*

》   MORE SCRIPTURES TO DIG

- As you study this scene, cut Jesus' disciples a little slack. So far in the book of Luke, his followers have seen him cast out demons and cure physical afflictions (**Luke 4:31-41**). He's healed a man who couldn't walk (**Luke 5:17-26**), and he even raised a widow's son from the dead (**Luke 7:11-16**). Before this scene, however, the disciples hadn't seen Jesus apply his power to nature—to something nonliving. Given their reaction to the miracle he performs, you've got to wonder if they just wanted him to help bail water. We have the advantage of knowing the whole truth about Jesus. We can access the entire Bible to see who God is and why we can count on him.

- Jesus keeps pressing his disciples to figure him out. Just a bit after this scene, he asks them an all-important question: "Who do you say I am?" Read about it in **Luke 9:18-20**, then catch more detail in **Matthew 16:13-20**. If you want to be crazed in your passion for talking with God, the secret is getting to know him and learning to trust him more and more.

Many people think teenagers aren't capable of much. But Zach Hunter is proving those people wrong. He's only fifteen, but he's working to end slavery in the world—and he's making changes that affect millions of people. Find out how Zach is making a difference and how you can make changes in the things that you see wrong with our world.

Be the Change
Your Guide to Freeing Slaves and Changing the World
Zach Hunter
RETAIL $9.99
ISBN 0-310-27756-6

Most teenagers think that being a Christian means doing the right thing, but figuring out what the "right thing" is can be a challenge. It's difficult for students to tell the difference between God's plan for them and what other Christians say is God's plan for them. Author Mark Matlock will guide your students through God's Word to help them figure out what God really wants from them.

What Does God Want from Me?
Understanding God's Desire for Your Life
Mark Matlock
RETAIL $9.99
ISBN 0-310-25815-4

Visit www.invertbooks.com or your local bookstore.

If you've ever wondered if God is really there and listening, if you're good enough, or what's so great about heaven, you're not alone. We all have had personal questions, but the answers are often harder to come by. In this book, you'll discover how to navigate your big questions, and what the answers mean for your life and faith.

Living with Questions
Dale Fincher
RETAIL $9.99
ISBN 0-310-27664-0

Love This! contains real-life stories of people like you who've found ways to love their neighbors. It will challenge you to make a difference in your world by loving people who are often ignored or unloved—the homeless, the addicted, the elderly, those of different races, even your enemies—and show you tangible ways you can demonstrate that love.

Love This!
Learning to Make It a Way of Life, Not Just a Word
Andy Braner
RETAIL $12.99
ISBN 0-310-27380-3

Visit www.invertbooks.com or your local bookstore.